Laptop Lifestyle

VOLUME 4

From Dream to Reality - The Online Success Planner and Workbook

Christopher King

Laptop Lifestyle

VOLUME 4

From Dream to Reality -
The Online Success Planner and Workbook

by

Christopher King

Suite 264

2 Toronto St.

Toronto, ON Canada

M5C 2B5

For more information on this series,
please visit us on the web at
www.PrepareToQuit.com

~ TABLE OF CONTENTS ~

Important Message from the Author 5

Introduction 7

Section One: Quick Start Guide To Making Money Online 9

    Chapter 1: Choosing A Product................................11

    Chapter 2: Offering A "Free Tour" 17

    Chapter 3: Promoting Your Chosen Product With A Salesletter................31

    Chapter 4: Creating A Web Site For Your Salesletter..................43

    Chapter 5: Getting Traffic To Your Site.....................51

Section Two: How To Create And Sell Your Own Products.................59

    Chapter 6: What Will Your eBook Be About?...................61

    Chapter 7: Choosing The Format Of Your eBook 67

    Chapter 8: Writing Your eBook 73

    Chapter 9: Promoting Your eBook 83

Section Three: Bonus Internet Marketing Techniques 89

    Chapter 10: Borrowing From Other Internet Marketers 91

    Chapter 11: Developing Your Own Unique Approach 105

    Chapter 12: The Power of Joint Ventures..................... 109

    Chapter 13: Putting Together A Joint Venture................. 115

    Chapter 14: Making Joint Ventures Pay Off For Months To Come 127

    Chapter 15: More Money-Making Opportunities 133

Conclusion... 137

LISTEN UP BECAUSE THIS IS IMPORTANT!

This book, Volume 4 of the Laptop Lifestyle series, has been designed as a companion guide to Volumes 1-3, which go into much greater detail about what it takes to make money online. This book is a supplement to the information in Volumes 1-3 and has been designed to help you create a custom business using that information.

I highly recommend that you read the other books in the Laptop Lifestyle series before you go through this workbook. Skipping this foundation will likely be a frustrating experience that I'd like to see you avoid. :)

To your success!

Christopher King

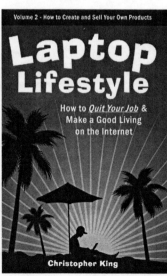

INTRODUCTION

ARE YOU READY TO LEAD A LAPTOP LIFESTYLE?

If you bought this workbook, and the other volumes in the series (which you will need to make best use of this workbook), my guess is you are serious about making the transition from having a 9 to 5 job and embrace the flexibility and financial gain that comes with creating a business online.

When it comes to making money online, there are a myriad of income streams you can choose from. Within the Laptop Lifestyle series, the focus in on affiliate marketing (promoting other people's products and getting paid for each sale you make) and creating your own information products for you, and others, to sell.

Right after you make the choice to become an affiliate marketer and product creator, you're hit with a lot of decisions to make. What niche will you sell in? Whose product will you promote? How will you promote it? What kind of product will you create? Who can you do joint ventures with?

Every step can be a bit overwhelming. That's why I created this workbook. Not only did I want the chance to expand upon what I wrote in the Laptop

Lifestyle series, but also I wanted you to have a book in which you could record all your ideas and the results you found when doing your research.

Making "mental notes" or scattering your ideas on scraps of unorganized papers won't bring your closer to your success. Keeping your ideas in one organized book will. Not only can you reference your notes quickly, but you can also go back and read the advice and suggestions I gave you to help inspire your ideas. All you need is in one place.

Often times, we buy a workbook with every intention of putting it to use. But the days go on and the workbook sits on our desk unused. I encourage you to have a different experience with this book. The more you use it, the more you will be motivated to take action on your ideas. Once you know what direction you want to go in, it won't take you long to move forward.

This is an exciting time for you! This is the beginning of your Internet business. You are about to change your life and enhance the lives of those you love. It is my honor to play a role in helping you do that.

Now, let's start making money!

SECTION ONE

QUICK START GUIDE TO MAKING MONEY ONLINE

As you read in *Quick Start Guide to Making Money Online*, one of the quickest, and easiest ways to start making money on the Web is by promoting products created by other people. Once you find a product you would like to promote, the product creator will give you something called an "affiliate link." You can place this link on your Web site, your blog, within emails, and anywhere else you think potential buyers would see it. When someone clicks on that link and makes a purchase, you receive a percentage of the sale.

Many people are making a full-time living doing this. They call themselves "affiliate marketers." You, too, can become an affiliate marketer. The first step is to choose what products you would like to promote.

At first, the idea of going for only the products that pay out a high affiliate commission per sale or a top-selling product might seem like a logical choice. However, if you are new to affiliate marketing, choosing products you have an interest in, no matter what the affiliate commission is, would be a better option. This way, when you begin promoting the product, you will have an easier time creating content (such as blog posts, articles, emails, etc) to promote the product. Also, your buyers will sense your knowingness and feel as though you are genuinely passing along good information to them rather than just trying to sell them something.

CHAPTER ONE

CHOOSING A PRODUCT

Now it's time to choose a product to promote.

What 10 things do you know a lot about?

1. _____

2. _____

3. _____

4. _____

5. _____

6. _____

7. _____

8. _____

9. _____

10. _____

What 10 topics would you be willing to take a few weeks to learn and then teach others?

1. _____

2. _____

3. _____

4. _____

5. _____

6. _____

7. _____

8. _____

9. _____

10. _____

Now that you have a list of 20 ideas, it's time to see if any of your ideas (or *niches*, as they are called in the Internet marketing world) have affiliate programs.

When it comes to a wide variety of products and a trusted affiliate program, Amazon.com is the best place to start your search. While the commissions are typically high, money is money and you can make a little here and there by introducing people to Amazon products using your affiliate link.

Clickbank.com and CJ.com are also sites on which you should search for products. You can also do a Google search of your niche and seek out independent companies that have an affiliate program. More often than not, if you scroll to the bottom of their Web site, they will have a very small link entitled "Affiliates" for you to click on to get more information.

As an example, let's say one of your ideas/niches was fly fishing. Do a Google search using "fly fishing affiliate program" and see what comes up. Several sites do. One of them even offers 50% percent commission on sales you bring to their site.

Now it's time to do your own research. Do a search using the niches you are interested in and write down the sites you find:

1. _____

2. _____

3. _____

4. _____

5. _____

6. _____

7. _____

8. _____

9. _____

10. _____

It's time to narrow done your list of niches. Let's say one of the niches you came up with is underwater basket weaving. Then you did a search and found one or two Web sites that have affiliate programs for underwater basket-weaving products. So far, so good. But let's be honest; chances are, not a lot of people are looking for information or products in this niche. It's just not that popular. It's time for you to go through your list. Keep the niches that are popular and leave behind the ones that aren't.

How do you know what people are searching for?

- Use Google Keyword Tool to see how many people were searching for your niche.
- Use WordTracker.com to see keyword search results from all the major search engines.

No matter what keyword tool you use, you'll get an immediate idea of which niches are hot and which ones you will want to leave behind.

Once you do your keyword search, write down the niches you will want to keep:

1. _____

2. _____

3. _____

4. _____

5. _____

6. _____

7. _____

8. _____

9. _____

10. _____

CHAPTER TWO

OFFERING A "FREE TOUR"

I would hope, at this point, you have at least one niche in mind that you would like to begin promoting.

Once that decision is made, your attention will probably turn to building a Web site or how you will get traffic to your Web site. Before we delve into both, there is something else to consider: How you will entice people to buy the product you are promoting.

These days, no matter what you are selling, you are competing with many other affiliate marketers who are doing the exact same thing you are and, possibly promoting the exact same products. So, how do you stand out from all your other competitors to win the trust of the buyer?

You offer them a free, valuable enticement that your competitors do not.

You can get creative with the enticement you give. It could be an exclusive "how to" video you created or an audio recording of an interview you did with an expert in the niche you are promoting. The point of offering an enticement is two-fold. You want to give people a reason to feel good about buying from you and you want to have a vehicle to promote your affiliate link.

One of the best enticements that has been used for years is what I like to call a "free tour" or, as it more commonly known, an "e-course." I suggest creating a five-lesson e-course that both educates and entertains. Remember, as I said in *Quick Start Guide to Making Money Online*, there is a big difference between a "road map" and a "tour guide." People can't resist personalized assistance, personalized training, and personalized interaction.

Let's say the niche you have chosen is dog training. The product you have chosen to promote is an ebook on crate training your dog. Your e-course could be five lessons on how to introduce your dog to the crate. Each lesson could include stories of your own experiences, suggestions on choosing the best crate and how to deal with the emotions that come with having to put your dog in a crate. In other words, offer much more than step-by-step instruction on how to perform the task of crate training.

YOUR LESSON PLAN:

Lesson 1:

This lesson will be about:

_____

_____

_____

_____

Action steps the reader will take or homework they will do after reading the lesson:

1. _____

2. _____

3. _____

4. _____

5. _____

Links to any other free resources:

1. _____

2. _____

3. _____

Critical points within the lesson where you will place the offer for the product you are promoting:

1. _____

2. _____

3. _____

4. _____

5. _____

Lesson 2:

This lesson will be about:

_____

_____

_____

_____

_____

Action steps the reader will take or homework they will do after reading the lesson:

1. _____

2. _____

3. _____

4. _____

5. _____

Links to any other free resources:

1. _____

2. _____

3. _____

Critical points within the lesson where you will place the offer for the product you are promoting:

1. _____

2. _____

3. _____

4. _____

5. _____

Lesson 3:

This lesson will be about:

_____

_____

_____

_____

Action steps the reader will take or homework they will do after reading the lesson:

1. _____

2. _____

3. _____

4. _____

5. _____

Links to any other free resources:

1. _____

2. _____

3. _____

Critical points within the lesson where you will place the offer for the product you are promoting:

1. _____

2. _____

3. _____

4. _____

5. _____

Lesson 4:

This lesson will be about:

_____

_____

_____

_____

_____

Action steps the reader will take or homework they will do after reading the lesson:

1. _____

2. _____

3. _____

4. _____

5. _____

Links to any other free resources:

1. _____

2. _____

3. _____

Critical points within the lesson where you will place the offer for the product you are promoting:

1. _____

2. _____

3. _____

4. _____

5. _____

Lesson 5:

This lesson will be about:

_____

_____

_____

_____

_____

Action steps the reader will take or homework they will do after reading the lesson:

1. _____

2. _____

3. _____

4. _____

5. _____

Links to any other free resources:

1. _____

2. _____

3. _____

Critical points within the lesson where you will place the offer for the product you are promoting:

1. _____

2. _____

3. _____

4. _____

5. _____

With the Free Tour Comes a Free Incentive

Another way you can winner over potential buyers and get more sales than your competition is to, at the end of your e-course, offer a free incentive. This goes above and beyond the five lessons you have sent to them. Now that you have their attention, and hopefully their trust, if they buy from you they get an extra special bonus.

(Keep in mind, these bonuses should only be offered when you are promoting a product for which you will receive a decent commission – $25 or more.)

The bonus you offer can take any form you like. It can range from video training, to creating customized graphics, to doing a 15-minute coaching session, to an exclusive ebook. The bonus has to be have a perceived high value and be something no one else but you could offer.

List ten things you could offer as a bonus incentive:

1. _____

2. _____

3. _____

4. _____

5. _____

6. _____

7. _____

8. _____

9. _____

10. _____

CHAPTER THREE

PROMOTING YOUR CHOSEN PRODUCT WITH A SALESLETTER

These days, we may have many ways to try and get the attention of potential buyers, but one method that remains tried and true is the classic salesletter. The long-form salesletter makes just as much of an impact today as it did decades ago when it was used in direct marketing through postal mail.

It is within the salesletter that you win potential buyers over, not by promoting the product you are selling, but by selling them on the free content you offering (your e-course and your bonus). Once they give you their email address, not only will you have the chance to tell them about the product you are currently promoting, you will have the chance to sell them other products in the future – including your own if you choose to make the leap from someone who sells other people's products to creating and selling your own.

There's no need to feel overwhelmed when it comes to writing a salesletter. You don't have to be an expert copywriter, but you do need to follow a few simple steps.

In *Quick Start Guide to Making Money Online,* I explain more in depth what each part of the salesletter is and how to write each part most effectively. Within this workbook, I want you to write down your ideas for each.

Headline

Do a search on the Web and look at other salesletters. Write down 10 headlines that got your attention:

1. _____

2. _____

3. _____

4. _____

5. _____

6. _____

7. _____

8. _____

9. _____

10. _____

Now, make those headlines your own by changing them up to fit your offer:

1. _____

2. _____

3. _____

4. _____

5. _____

6. _____

7. _____

8. _____

9. _____

10. _____

Subheader

Same thing with the subheader. Find 10 subheaders you think make an impact on the reader:

1. _____

2. _____

3. _____

4. _____

5. _____

6. _____

7. _____

8. _____

9. _____

10. _____

Make these subheaders your own by changing them up to fit your offer:

1. _____

2. _____

3. _____

4. _____

5. _____

6. _____

7. _____

8. _____

9. _____

10. _____

Opening Paragraph

Come up with 10 sentences that will captivate the reader and be so irresistible that they will want to read on:

1. _____

_____

_____

2. _____

_____

_____

3. _____

_____

_____

4. _____

_____

_____

5. _____

_____

_____

6. _____

_____

_____

7. _____

_____

_____

8. _____

_____

_____

9. _____

_____

10. _____

_____

Bullet Points

List 10 of the strongest benefits your free e-course and your free incentive have. Answer the age-old question, "What's in it for me?":

1. _____

2. _____

3. _____

4. _____

5. _____

6. _____

7. _____

8. _____

9. _____

10. _____

Testimonials

Testimonials take your incentive from "just another offer" to one with some punch. Your offer works. It helps. It changes. It empowers. Whatever it's supposed to do, it does it – and you have people lined up to prove it.

Make a list of people you can ask for a testimonial:

1. _____

2. _____

3. _____

4. _____

5. _____

6. _____

7. _____

8. _____

9. _____

10. _____

Call To Action

Now that the reader is convinced they need your incentive, it's time to show them how they can get it. You simply want to explain to the reader what it takes to say "yes" and accept your offer.

Let them know that if they purchase whatever affiliate product you are offering, then they can grab your incentive at no cost to them.

Give them your affiliate link and explain what to do after they order to collect the freebie. Then, tell them to stop wasting time and get to it!

Write the first draft of your "call to action" below. Remember, give clear instructions on how the buyer can contact you with proof they made a purchase to receive their bonus:

_____

_____

_____

_____

_____

_____

_____

_____

_____

_____

_____

_____

_____

<hr>

CHAPTER FOUR

CREATING A WEB SITE FOR YOUR SALESLETTER

When it comes to creating a basic Web page which will contain your salesletter, keep these rules in mind:

- Have a professional layout design that is pleasing to the eyes.

- Use bulleted lists (like the one you are now reading) that make information easily available.

- Change fonts, colors or highlights to emphasize certain words and phrases in bold and italics and underline.

- Don't forget to use lots of white space.

- Use shaded backgrounds and/or bordered boxes to highlight important information, such as testimonials and research.

- Headlines should be noticeably larger and centered on your page in order to attract attention.

- If you can obtain permission from the owner of the affiliate program you are promoting, use the same, similar or portions of the Web page graphics of the product or service you are promoting as an affiliate. It creates a visual connection and helps maintain a seamless flow.

- Resist the temptation to get too clever with extra graphics. Instead, focus on a quick-loading page that is professionally designed with attractive graphics.

- Be typographically and grammatically accurate. Typos and grammar errors leave a bad impression with many people. It says, "If this person can't at least proofread his offer, how valuable can the offer be?" Have a professional editor proofread it for you. You want to make certain you don't send any warning signals that would discount your offer.

- As the old adage goes, "You never get a second chance to make a first impression." Make yours count. Choose a professional, fast-loading layout that is used as an extension of the offer itself. An attractive layout enhances your offer and is actually a very important part of the sales process.

There are key things you need to include with your salesletter. The first, and most important, is the email capture box. This is where the potential buyer will register to receive your free e-course. There are several companies that offer email marketing software and provide you with the HTML code you copy and then paste onto your salesletter Web page. Two of the most popular companies are Aweber.com and 1ShoppingCart.com.

Do a Google search to find three of these companies and write down the pros and cons for each:

Company #1

_____

Pros:

_____

_____

_____

Cons:

_____

_____

_____

Company #2

_____

Pros:

_____

_____

_____

Cons:

_____

_____

_____

Company #3

Pros:

Cons:

Exit Pop-Up Window

I'm sure you have been to a Web site and upon trying to leave it, a pop-up window appears. You may think they are annoying and intrusive, but they do work. The exit pop-up window is your last chance to convince the potential buyer to reconsider signing up for your offer before they leave the site (and may never return).

What would you say to those people to change their mind and get them to sign up for your e-course? Write down your ideas:

1. _____

2. _____

3. _____

4. _____

5. _____

6. _____

7. _____

8. _____

9. _____

10. _____

Graphics

It's one thing to tell people about a freebie they will receive, but giving them a visual of it makes the offer that much more powerful. Create a graphic that looks similar to a book cover to help promote your offer.

In the lines below, brainstorm what you would like the graphic to look like:

_____

_____

_____

_____

_____

CHAPTER FIVE

GETTING TRAFFIC TO YOUR SITE

Quick Start Guide to Making Money Online is a book is about "incentive marketing" and not "traffic generation," so I'm not going to cover promotion in great detail. However, I do want to give you a few ideas on how to quickly get the word out about your new offer.

Within this workbook, I encourage you to research your options, make notes, and then decide which traffic-generating methods would work best for you.

Solo Mailing

(For those who already have a mailing list)

Pros:

_____

_____

_____

_____

Cons:

_____

_____

_____

_____

Pay-Per-Click Advertising

Pros:

_____

_____

_____

_____

Cons:

_____

_____

_____

Joint-Venture Mailing

(Partnering with someone who has a mailing list)

Pros:

_____

_____

_____

_____

Cons:

_____

_____

_____

_____

Using Social Media

(Giving out your link on sites like Facebook, Twitter, StumbleUpon, Tumblr, etc.)

Pros:

_____

_____

_____

_____

Cons:

_____

_____

_____

_____

Posting on Forums

Pros:

_____

_____

_____

_____

Cons:

_____

_____

_____

_____

Article Marketing

(Writing short articles that contain a link to your site and posting them on article directories, such as EzineArticles.com)

Pros:

_____

_____

_____

_____

Cons:

_____

_____

_____

_____

Other ideas:

1. _____

2. _____

3. _____

4. _____

5. _____

6. _____

7. _____

8. _____

9. _____

10. _____

SECTION TWO

HOW TO CREATE AND SELL YOUR OWN PRODUCTS

Being an affiliate marketer can be very lucrative. There are many people who have multiple streams of income garnered through the promotion of other people's products. While some people are satisfied to stop there, I would encourage you to move to the next level of Internet marketing: creating and selling your own ebooks.

CHAPTER SIX

WHAT WILL YOUR EBOOK BE ABOUT?

As I wrote in *How to Create and Sell Your Own Products*, once you have created a free bonus, the salesletter, and a Web site to promote your offer, set up a mailing list to collect contact information from your Web site visitors. This is more cost- and time-efficient than spending the majority of your time searching for new buyers to come to your site because you can offer new products to the people who sign up for your mailing list!

One of the most popular niches is weight loss. Let's say you chose to promote one of the best selling weight loss ebooks on Clickbank.com. Play on the marketing savvy of the ebook's creator by giving people a bonus they won't likely refuse: a free teleseminar with you and the ebook's creator through which the customers' weight loss questions can be answered. Even if only 100 people sign up,, those are still 100 people to whom you can continue to market. During the teleseminar they would have the chance to hear your voice and get to know you. You'd then stay in touch once a week to give them weight loss tips.

While you are keeping in touch with them, you could write your own weight loss ebook. As an example, you could offer a "10-Day Green Smoothie Cleanse" filled with instructions and recipes. You could offer it exclusively to the 100 people on your mailing list, selling it for $27. Even if only 20 people bought it after you sent out your first email, that's still $540 income. And keep in mind, new people will be joining your mailing list all the time. You will have many opportunities to sell your ebook.

But maybe weight loss isn't a niche you want to get into. After all, it is extremely competitive. So what niche do you want to explore and how can you expand upon what other people have already done?

How do you decide if a niche market will make you money? Make sure it possesses at least two of these characteristics:

1. It is actively searched for on the Internet

2. There is already competition in the marketplace

3. You find it interesting or enjoyable

List 10 niches that fit the characteristics listed above:

1. _____

2. _____

3. _____

4. _____

5. _____

6. _____

7. _____

8. _____

9. _____

10. _____

Now it's time to dig a bit deeper to find out what topics within your niche are worth pursuing. Earlier in the book, I suggested you do keyword research. This time, we are going to check out: MyGoals.com, SoYouWanna.com, and eHow.com to see what people are looking for. You will be using these sites to generate ideas for your ebook, not copying and using any of the content found on these sites.

MyGoals.com:

Look over your list of niches. Visit MyGoals.com and do a search of the category your niche falls into. As an example, if your niche is "Home Improvement" check out the many sub-categories this niche has. One of them is "Pond and Waterfall." Someone listed "Keep a pond clean" as one of their goals. Can you see how a short, instructional ebook on this topic would be needed by those who have a pond?

Write down the ideas you get from visiting MyGoals.com:

1. _____

2. _____

3. _____

4. _____

5. _____

6. _____

7. _____

8. _____

9. _____

10. _____

Write down 10 ebook ideas you get from SoYouWanna.com:

1. _____

2. _____

3. _____

4. _____

5. _____

6. _____

7. _____

8. _____

9. _____

10. _____

Write down 10 ebook ideas you get from eHow.com:

1. _____

2. _____

3. _____

4. _____

5. _____

6. _____

7. _____

8. _____

9. _____

10. _____

CHAPTER SEVEN

CHOOSING THE FORMAT OF YOUR EBOOK

While you can hire a ghostwriter to create your ebook, you may want to write the first one yourself. There are several formats you can choose from. See *How to Create and Sell Your Own Products* for more detailed descriptions of the ones I am about to list. Use this workbook to brainstorm ideas that come to mind when you think about each format and whether it would work for your ebook or not.

FORMAT OPTION 1
Answering Frequently Asked Questions (FAQ)

1. _____

2. _____

3. _____

4. _____

5. _____

6. _____

7. _____

8. _____

9. _____

10. _____

FORMAT OPTION 2
Writing a Step-by-Step Tutorial

1. _____

2. _____

3. _____

4. _____

5. _____

6. _____

7. _____

8. _____

9. _____

10. _____

FORMAT OPTION 3
Collection of Tips or Ways To Solve a Problem

1. _____

2. _____

3. _____

4. _____

5. _____

6. _____

7. _____

8. _____

9. _____

10. _____

FORMAT OPTION 4
Collection of Resources

1. _____

2. _____

3. _____

4. _____

5. _____

6. _____

7. _____

8. _____

9. _____

10. _____

FORMAT OPTION 5
Transcription of An Interview

1. _____

2. _____

3. _____

4. _____

5. _____

6. _____

7. _____

8. _____

9. _____

10. _____

CHAPTER EIGHT

WRITING YOUR EBOOK

Hopefully, at this point, you know what the topic of your ebook is going to be and the format you will use.

If you have never written anything as thorough as an ebook before, don't stress! Use a simple writing formula to get the project done:

Step 1: Write out a list of everything you want to share, even if they are just random ideas associated with your subject.

Step 2: For each thing you wrote in step one, write down research, examples, case studies, quotes, tips, resources and anything you can find.

Step 3: Take everything you have now and put it into a logical order, so your readers can understand it. For example, if you're writing a book on how to quit smoking, then make sure the part about "what to do after you quit" comes toward the end!

Step 4: Edit, edit, edit. Take out what doesn't need to be in there. Add more content to the sections that need further explanation.

What makes you different? Why should a customer buy from you instead of your competition? Are you faster, better, cheaper? Do you offer more, or maybe more for less? From the beginning, you need to find some way that separates you from the rest of the pack.

One of the most important things you can do is determine why someone should buy from you, and then work on providing that as you write.

What is your unique approach?

_____

_____

_____

_____

_____

_____

_____

_____

Beyond making money with your ebook, what other purpose do you have for writing it?

To stay focused on your objectives, have something that is waiting at the end of the journey. Keeping your objective in sight is much easier when you're excited about your work and strive to succeed at your goals. The great thing is that you're never too young or too old!

Even if you just want to be able to say to someone, "See, we told you we could do it," that's a valid purpose. One of the most satisfying things in life is to do something that someone told you couldn't be done.

Write down your purpose:

_____

_____

_____

_____

_____

_____

_____

_____

What is it that you want to share with those who download your ebook? This is an extremely important step and one that shouldn't be missed. If you don't write your objectives down, you will quickly lose sight of them. Keeping them in sight – literally, somewhere you can see them when you're working – will help you achieve them.

What are your objectives?

_____

_____

_____

_____

_____

_____

_____

_____

Choosing a title helps you organize the ideas that support the main theme of the ebook. You can also use the title to help you create your actual chapter headings.

Jot down some potential working titles for your ebook:

1. _____

_____

2. _____

_____

3. _____

_____

4. _____

_____

5. _____

_____

A thesis states the audience's main problem, and how your book is going to solve it. Basically, you are expanding upon the title of the ebook.

If "How to Become a Great Golfer" is the title, your thesis statement might be, "How to become a great golfer in less than an hour a day by following seven strategies of other successful golfers."

Everything you write should help accomplish what you state in your thesis. If it doesn't, then it doesn't belong in your ebook.

Write down your thesis:

_____

_____

_____

_____

_____

_____

_____

_____

_____

_____

_____

_____

_____

_____

_____

_____

_____

_____

It's time to write the opening of your ebook.

The power of curiosity is very compelling. People want to know. It is almost hypnotic. If you can use some kind of attention-grabbing opening sentence and/or opening paragraph to make the reader think, "I've got to find out what this is all about," then you've got them glued to your book for basically as long as you want. Well-written supporting paragraphs will have them reading until the very end.

Consider using these kinds of opening sentences that draw people deeper into your book:

- *"I bet you would have never guessed it."*

- *"I just couldn't believe it really happened."*

- *"No one could have predicted this."*

- *"All of the experts finally agreed on something."*

- *"99% gave the wrong answer when we asked this simple question."*

Brainstorm ideas for opening lines:

1. _____

2. _____

3. _____

4. _____

5. _____

6. _____

7. _____

8. _____

9. _____

10. _____

CHAPTER NINE

PROMOTING YOUR EBOOK

Once you have your ebook written and ready to sell, it's time to choose how you want to promote it. Like I wrote earlier, you can offer it exclusively to those who have signed up for your mailing list. But why not let everyone know about it?

In section one, we briefly covered creating a Web site and salesletter. We also considered a few ways to advertise your site. Here are a few more ways to get the word out about your ebook:

Joint Ventures

We'll be going more in depth with finding people to do joint ventures with in Section Three. For now, brainstorm and do some searching online to find people you could contact to ask if they would like to promote your ebook:

1. _____

2. _____

3. _____

4. _____

5. _____

6. _____

7. _____

8. _____

9. _____

10. _____

Forums

List the message boards and forums where your audience is known to participate and where you can promote your ebook each time you post:

1. _____

2. _____

3. _____

4. _____

5. _____

6. _____

7. _____

8. _____

9. _____

10. _____

Social Networking Sites

List the sites where you would like to create a profile and presence to help promote your ebook:

1. _____

2. _____

3. _____

4. _____

5. _____

6. _____

7. _____

8. _____

9. _____

10. _____

The "Thank You" Page of Your Mailing List

After someone signs up for your mailing list, they are taken to a confirmation page which you can customize into a thank you page. Write down the copy you would include on this page to entice them to buy your ebook:

_____

_____

_____

_____

_____

_____

_____

Final Tip

Why not combine your affiliate marketing with product creation? Within your ebook (either at the end or throughout the text), give the reader suggestions on products to check out that would help them even more. Always include your affiliate link to these products.

SECTION THREE

BONUS INTERNET MARKETING TECHNIQUES

Now that you have a taste of what affiliate marketing is all about as well how to create your own product, you'll want to put your focus on how to drive lots of traffic to your Web site and how to get people interested enough to follow through by either signing up for your mailing list or buying a product.

One of the most powerful ways to do this is by teaming up with other Internet marketers to do what is known as a "joint venture." The history of Internet marketing is filled with stories of people joining together to make tens of thousands of dollars by agreeing to do business together. Who's to say you can't do the same?

Finally, we will go over just a few more money-making tactics that will help you bring in even more income.

CHAPTER TEN

BORROWING FROM OTHER INTERNET MARKETERS

O ne of the best ways to learn how to amp up your marketing techniques is to study what other, very successful, marketers have done before you.

You don't want to copy what they have done. Instead, you want to borrow their techniques and make them your own.

One of the most important things to study is sales copy.

For now, I encourage you to check out two successful sales pages: StopYourDivorce.com and MagicOfMakingUp.com. Both products have generated multiple thousands of dollars in sales. Study the format of the sales copy and take notes of what you observe:

StopYourDivorce.com:

How are they using headlines?

_____

_____

_____

How long is the salesletter?

_____

_____

_____

What kind of language is it written in? (i.e., compelling words and phrases)

_____

_____

_____

What kind of format is being used? (bullet lists, highlighting, bold, italic)

_____

_____

_____

What is the opening sentence? Did it pull you into the letter? Why?

_____

_____

_____

How do they keep your attention as you read the salesletter?

_____

_____

_____

Do they use testimonials? How many? Where? Are they effective?

_____

_____

_____

How easy or hard is it to order the product?

_____

_____

_____

What kind of call to action is there? Is there a deadline?

_____

_____

_____

What about the offer makes you want to buy, or not buy?

_____

_____

_____

Is there any point that it gets boring? Why? What would you do differently?

_____

_____

_____

What makes the salesletter compelling to you? What could be better?

_____

_____

_____

MagicOfMakingUp.com:

How are they using headlines?

_____

_____

_____

How long is the salesletter?

_____

_____

_____

What kind of language is it written in? (i.e., compelling words and phrases)

_____

_____

_____

What kind of format is being used? (bullet lists, highlighting, bold, italic)

_____

_____

_____

What is the opening sentence? Did it pull you into the letter? Why?

_____

_____

_____

How do they keep your attention as you read the salesletter?

_____

_____

_____

Do they use testimonials? How many? Where? Are they effective?

_____

_____

_____

How easy or hard is it to order the product?

_____

_____

_____

What kind of call to action is there? Is there a deadline?

_____

_____

_____

What about the offer makes you want to buy, or not buy?

_____

_____

_____

Is there any point that it gets boring? Why? What would you do differently?

_____

_____

_____

What makes the salesletter compelling to you? What could be better?

_____

_____

_____

While you are visiting MagicOfMakingUp.com, sign up for their affiliate program. (The "Affiliate" link is at the bottom of the Web page.) Even if you have no interest in promoting this product, study how their affiliate program is set up to learn 1) what a professional and well-run affiliate program looks like and 2) how to get ideas for your own affiliate program ebooks and future infoproducts.

Write down answers to these questions:

How often are affiliates paid? How much are they paid?

_____

_____

_____

Is the program one-tier or multi-tier? Why?

_____

_____

_____

What kind of affiliate tracking is used for the affiliate program?

_____

_____

_____

What affiliate marketing materials are provided?

_____

_____

_____

Does the program have an affiliate training manual? What's in it?

_____

_____

_____

Is there a regular affiliate training newsletter published? What's in it?

_____

_____

_____

Where are the affiliate links being advertised?

_____

_____

_____

How is the owner recruiting new affiliates?

_____

_____

_____

CHAPTER ELEVEN

DEVELOPING YOUR OWN UNIQUE APPROACH

Once you have an understanding of how other marketers have created success and borrowed their techniques, there is one more thing for you to do: Go beyond what has already been done.

The question you need to ask yourself is: How can I add my own unique approach to an existing product?

The truth is, you can have the best sales copy and the best affiliate program, but if you aren't offering something that is just a little different than your competitors, buyers will lose interest.

As you think about making your ebook better, or begin planning your second one, answer the following questions:

How can you make your ebook different from other ebooks?

1. _____

2. _____

3. _____

How can you approach ebook sales in a unique way that will stand out from your competition?

1. _____

2. _____

3. _____

Is there a niche within your niche? Perhaps a specific segment or the market that you can focus on? Can you focus on a specific group, such as beginners (skill level) or senior citizens (age)?

1. _____

2. _____

3. _____

How about repackaging an ebook collection for that niche? For example, rewrite the salesletter and focus the ad copy toward specific references that apply to your niche (i.e., "Moms, here is something you can do to earn extra money while your toddler is taking her afternoon nap.").

1. _____

2. _____

3. _____

Is there something extra you can add to the collection to make it more niche friendly? If you're focusing on newbies, how about creating a short guide to answering their most asked questions? (i.e. How much time will it take? What equipment will I need? When can I expect to see results?, etc.)

1. _____

2. _____

3. _____

What kind of ebook hasn't been written that you see a need for, or that people are asking for?

1. _____

2. _____

3. _____

CHAPTER TWELVE

THE POWER OF JOINT VENTURES

In less than one year's time, I went from an unknown online to a Web marketing success. How did that happen? And, more importantly, how can you use the same tool I used to jump-start your own online business?

It all began with a joint venture, a partnership in which two different parties combine their individual resources for a mutually beneficial project.

For example: People have a resource in a product, but are limited in their contacts. I have a lot of contacts and am open to promoting the right offer. So, I promote their offer and keep a percentage of the sales. We both benefit in ways that would be impossible on our own.

I was an unknown. I didn't have any contacts. No one even knew my name. I wanted my potential partners to send a solo mailing to their entire list of subscribers to promote my new product. But who would want to promote it for me?

- I sent out offers for a joint venture. In exchange for their solo mailing, I offered:

  To allow them to customize the solo mailing with their affiliate link. Any sales that came in would automatically earn them a 50 percent commission. This gave them a stake in it. There was profit to be made!

- 100 percent free reprint rights to an ebook I wrote and was currently selling online. They could continue selling it long after the solo mailing was completed.

- A free copy of an incredible Internet marketing course I had purchased reprint rights to. I spent $600 to buy the rights and the course was selling for $29.97.

- A solo mailing to my own small but growing list of subscribers. They could promote anything they wanted to my list (as long as it wasn't illegal or immoral).

Now, how do you think this joint venture offer went over?

It was a huge success. Literally in less than 48 hours, the sales began to come pouring in. I sold thousands of dollars in memberships because of this project. And, it jump-started an entire landslide of profits because of a system I had in place.

You can duplicate this success with the power of joint venture marketing.

The question you may be asking yourself is, where do I find people to do joint ventures with?

There are three resources I recommend:

1. Do a Google search.

Who's ranking in the top 20 in keyword searches that would work well for your joint venture? Let's say I sell pets, and I want to put together a joint venture with those who sell pet supplies. I visit Google and do a search for "pet supplies." I could also search for more specific things like bird cages, cat food, dog obedience training videos, grooming supplies, aquariums, pet identification tags, etc.

I make a list of the top 20 Web sites found there. These are my contacts. I visit each and learn something about the site. Is it right for my project? Do they already sell pets? Does it appear to be professionally run? Is there contact information available?

If it looks like a good match for my joint venture proposal, then I find the name and email address of the contact person.

Now, do your own Google search. Write down what you find:

1. _____

2. _____

3. _____

4. _____

5. _____

2. Contact ezine publishers.

There are dozens of ezine directories online where you can find categorized listings of newsletters, their publishers and all pertinent contact information.

Begin your joint venture project by approaching ezine publishers who participate in ad swaps (also known as *ad exchanges*). They are already open to the idea of a joint venture, after all, an ad exchange is the simplest form of joint venture marketing. You'll find many of them willing, if not eager, to participate.

Search ezine directories and write down who would be a good match for you:

1. _____

2. _____

3. _____

4. _____

5. _____

3. Seek out the ClickBank.com achievers.

You will need to visit ClickBank's Marketplace, a categorical directory of their active account holders, and search for categories and sub-categories that are compatible with your joint venture proposal. Upon arriving at the sub-category pages of account listings, you will want to begin at the top and work your way down the index. ClickBank has a formula for how it ranks the accounts, primarily based on actual sales. Those that rank high in the categories and sub-categories are great potential partners.

Spend time at Clickbank.com taking note of product creators who are making high sales. Write down who would be a good match for you:

1. _____

2. _____

3. _____

4. _____

5. _____

CHAPTER THIRTEEN

PUTTING TOGETHER A JOINT VENTURE

n the book *Bonus Internet Marketing Techniques* I list 10 types of joint ventures you could put together. Read over each one and write down the pros and cons for each as they apply to your offer:

The "Lopsided" Ad Exchange

Pros:

1. _____

2. _____

3. _____

Cons:

1. _____

2. _____

3. _____

The "Everybody Wins" Contest

Pros:

1. _____

2. _____

3. _____

Cons:

1. _____

2. _____

3. _____

The "To Be Continued" Article Series

Pros:

1. _____

2. _____

3. _____

Cons:

1. _____

2. _____

3. _____

The "They're Leaving Anyway" Pop-up Swap

Pros:

1. _____

2. _____

3. _____

Cons:

1. _____

2. _____

3. _____

The "I'd Like to Thank My Co-Author" ecourse

Pros:

1. _____

2. _____

3. _____

Cons:

1. _____

2. _____

3. _____

The "Brand Name" Manuals

Pros:

1. _____

2. _____

3. _____

Cons:

1. _____

2. _____

3. _____

The "2-Minute Profits" License Trade

Pros:

1. _____

2. _____

3. _____

Cons:

1. _____

2. _____

3. _____

The "100% Free Advertising" Article Publication

Pros:

1. _____

2. _____

3. _____

Cons:

1. _____

2. _____

3. _____

The "Manual Makeover" 2-Hour Product Creation

Pros:

1. _____

2. _____

3. _____

Cons:

1. _____

2. _____

3. _____

The "Because You Know Him/Her" Pricing Trick

Pros:

1. _____

2. _____

3. _____

Cons:

1. _____

2. _____

3. _____

CHAPTER FOURTEEN

MAKING JOINT VENTURES PAY OFF FOR MONTHS TO COME

One of the biggest problems with most joint ventures is that people put together a super offer, and it works like a charm, but it's a one-time shot. They earn their money and then move on to something else.

With just a bit of careful planning, that same joint venture can be producing an ever-increasing income for months – and even years – to come.

Your joint venture must have a purpose.

Ask yourself one very simple question:

What do you want to accomplish with your joint venture? Write down your answers:

1. _____

2. _____

3. _____

Of course, the overwhelming answer I receive is "make a lot of money." Perhaps to your surprise, that is NOT the right goal. Granted, an increase in sales is a secondary goal; but there are three goals you need to aim for:

1. Building your mailing list

2. Securing lifetime customers

3. Recruiting new affiliates and partners

Build Your Mailing List

There are many things you can offer to entice people to sign up for your mailing list. Earlier in the workbook, we went over creating an ecourse. You could also offer a weekly newsletter, an audio recording, or a free report.

List five things you would like to offer your mailing list:

1. _____

2. _____

3. _____

4. _____

5. _____

Think Viral

How do you get lifetime customers and a lot of them?

You will want your joint venture to spread much farther than the project itself. Basically, you want it to spread like a virus. You create some kind of tool that will allow your marketing to grow and continue to spread on its own, without your personal interaction with any of the end users.

You can do this by doing such things as promoting your own ebook and giving it away to people while allowing them to include their own affiliate link. Rather than them having to write free content to give away to their mailing list, you do it for them. In return, you get sales from their promotion and they get commission for those sales. You can also sell the reprint rights to your ebook and allow people to use it without them making any changes to the content.

Write down five ways you can allow your marketing to grow beyond the initial joint venture:

1. _____

2. _____

3. _____

4. _____

5. _____

Work the Backend

I've said it before: it is much easier to sell to an existing customer than it is to seek out new customers. If you have a satisfied customer, it is only logical that they would be interested in purchasing additional, related products from you. The "backend" is any additional offer beyond the initial one.

Have you noticed that for many $19.97 products there is a $97 software tool you can buy in order to better use that $19.97 product? That's a backend. If you can buy reprint rights to that software tool for $697, that's another backend.

So, you've got to make that offer and have it in place before your joint venture project even begins. Whether you promote an affiliate program, your own products or a product you have purchased reprint rights to, you need to have your backend offer in place.

Earlier in the book, I mentioned how placing offers within a pop-up exit window and also the thank you page are both good marketing tools. The welcome email and the follow-up email you send to new mailing list subscribers are also good places to make backend offers.

List five tools you can use to make backend offers:

1. _____

2. _____

3. _____

4. _____

5. _____

CHAPTER FIFTEEN

MORE MONEY-MAKING OPPORTUNITIES

I deally, especially when you just starting out as an Internet marketer, you want to have many income streams. As I have mentioned, creating your own products is one of the best long-term income streams you can create for yourself. As someone who is going to also do affiliate marketing, the absolute best products to promote are the ones for which people make a monthly payment.

Once someone signs up for a service, you get a monthly affiliate commission as long as they continue to use it

You can find these sites via search engines, Clickbank.com, forums, and CJ.com.

Here are a few of the most common services from which you can earn a monthly income. Do a search and choose the Web sites you would like to promote:

Web hosts:

1. _____

2. _____

3. _____

Ad-tracking services:

1. _____

2. _____

3. _____

Autoresponders:

1. _____

2. _____

3. _____

Mailing list services:

1. _____

2. _____

3. _____

Affiliate program management

1. _____

2. _____

3. _____

Ultimate eBusiness management

(offers all-in-one autoresponders, mailing lists, ad tracking, affiliate program management, surveys/polls and pop-up windows service)

1. _____

2. _____

3. _____

Membership sites:

1. _____

2. _____

3. _____

~ CONCLUSION ~

There is really only one thing that separates those who are successful at making money online and those who are not: those who are successful at implementing their ideas.

At one time or another, we all get caught up in researching a niche, in not wanting to release something until it is perfect, and trying to figure out how to make money in a way that doesn't involve a lot of time or risk.

But the truth is, if you are serious about wanting to have a laptop lifestyle, you have to get focused and get to work. One day, you'll have your money-making systems in place and will be generating enough income that you can hire people to do the work for you. But as someone who is just beginning, you need to put in the time and effort.

It is my hope that you will make good use of all the ideas you came up with and all the resources you found online while using this workbook.

Right now, you are planting seeds. The remarkable thing about the Internet is that planted seeds can start sprouting within weeks, days, or even hours (if you send out one email to your mailing list). So have the courage to put yourself out there. Trust your gut when it comes to picking a good niche. Know that you have the ability to create good content people need and want. Most of all, don't be afraid to ask others if they would like to partner with you.

I wish you the greatest success.

Christopher King

PrepareToQuit.com

~ NOTES ~

~ NOTES ~

LaVergne, TN USA
12 November 2010

204575LV00001B/60/P